COOL PUZZLES FOR KIDS

Sharpen your pencils and get puzzling!

W9-CEA-737

ARCTURUS

ARCTURUS

This edition published in 2013 by Arcturus Publishing Limited
26/27 Bickels Yard, 151–153 Bermondsey Street,
London SE1 3HA

ISBN: 978-1-84837-631-1
CH001575EN
Supplier 03, Date 0413, Print Run 2659

Text and illustration: Small World Design

Printed in China

Contents

Puzzles 4

Answers 118

Clackety-clack

Which of these snappy suspects is the odd one out?

Boats ahoy

Can you find five different types of boat using the letters in each word wheel? We've given you the first letter of each word to start you off.

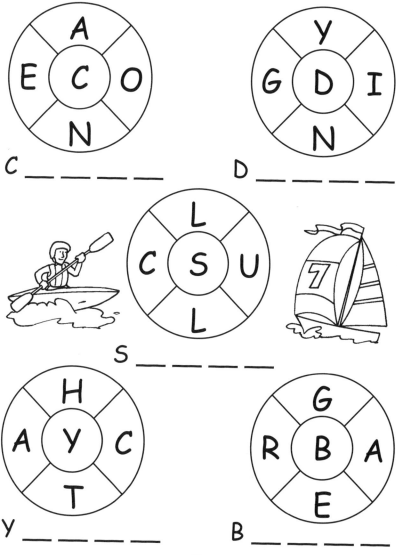

C _ _ _ _ _

D _ _ _ _ _

S _ _ _ _ _

Y _ _ _ _

B _ _ _ _ _

Woof! Woof!

Unscramble the letters to find four breeds of dog.

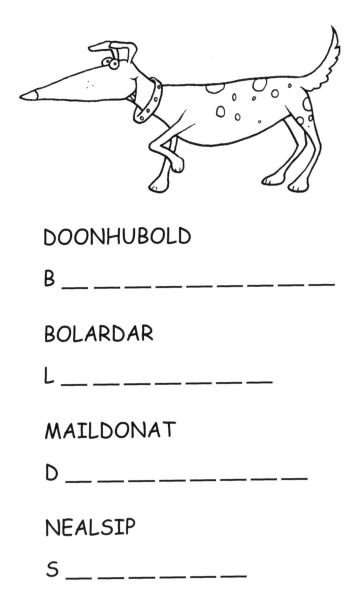

DOONHUBOLD

B __ __ __ __ __ __ __ __ __

BOLARDAR

L __ __ __ __ __ __ __

MAILDONAT

D __ __ __ __ __ __ __ __

NEALSIP

S __ __ __ __ __ __ __

Hungry frog

Finish the picture and draw the frog catching a fly!

Blast off!

Zoom off into the universe and find these planets, dwarfs and stars hidden in the wordsearch.

NEPTUNE   MERCURY
JUPITER   URANUS
SATURN   VENUS
PLUTO   EARTH
MARS   SIRIUS
POLE   MIRA

```
K V G O J R P G S M
N E P T U N E F I E
V N L H P Z M A R R
I U H D I Q Z F I C
O S S A T U R N U U
P I D J E M J Z S R
L N S U R A N U S Y
U P O L E K B L X B
T C E A R T H E A M
O M I R A Y M A R S
```

In class

All of these school-themed words have been split into two syllables. Connect the two halves to complete each word.

pen	ons
home	ground
white	pack
class	cher
tea	board
play	cil
back	work
less	room

Is this the right plaice?

Which shadow exactly matches this funky fish.

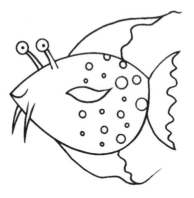

Horse sense

Start by crossing out the letter 'O' and then delete
alternate letters as you work your way through the list.
The remaining letters will reveal a famous book!

OBIL NARC EKUB

LEFAN USTRY

— — — — —

— — — — — —

Find the key

Follow the trails to find out which key opens the padlock.

Animal antics

Read the clues and complete the words using only vowels.

G __ R __ F F __   tallest land animal

C __ M __ L   a desert animal

C H __ __ T __ H   fast big cat

__ __ R D V __ R K   ant eater

K __ N G __ R __ __   Australian jumper

B __ B __ __ N   type of monkey

P __ N D __   black and white bear

M __ __ S __   a type of large deer

What's in the wardrobe?

Count the number of letters in each word,
and then fit them into the crossword grid.

TIE   SOCK   JEANS   JACKET

HAT   COAT   PYJAMAS   GLOVES

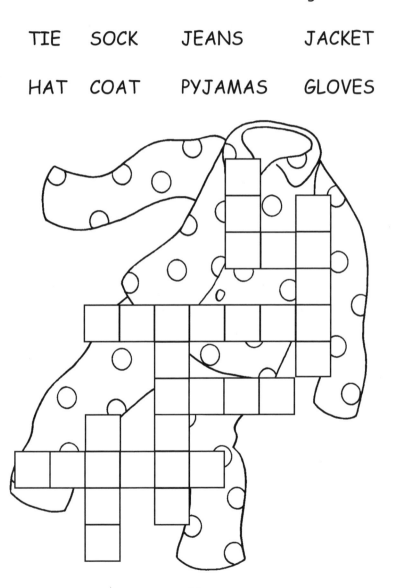

Flower power!

Which two flowers are exactly the same?

Joined up words

Join the words with the pictures to create four new words.

horse

honey

flower

paint

Write the new words here.

_____   _____

_____   _____

Knight knight!

Use the word square to crack the code and name one of King Arthur's knights.

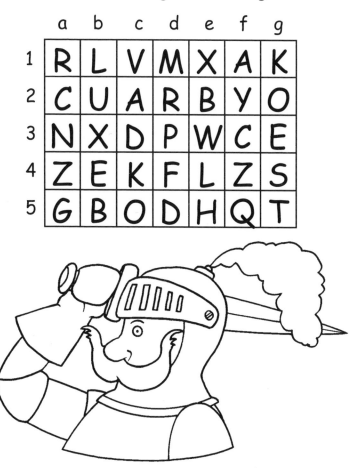

	a	b	c	d	e	f	g
1	R	L	V	M	X	A	K
2	C	U	A	R	B	Y	O
3	N	X	D	P	W	C	E
4	Z	E	K	F	L	Z	S
5	G	B	O	D	H	Q	T

Fill in the squares to name the knight.

1b   2c   3a   3f   4b   4e   5c   5g

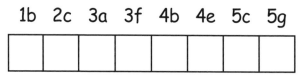

Ants in your pants!

Guide the anteater's sticky tongue through the maze so he can slurp up all the ants.

Vroom-vroom

One of these speedy racers is different to the others – can you spot which one it is?

Big top

It's a tall order to spot six differences between this picture and the one on the facing page!

Cock-a-doodle-baa

Unscramble the letters to find two types of bird in the first puzzle, and two farm animals in the second.

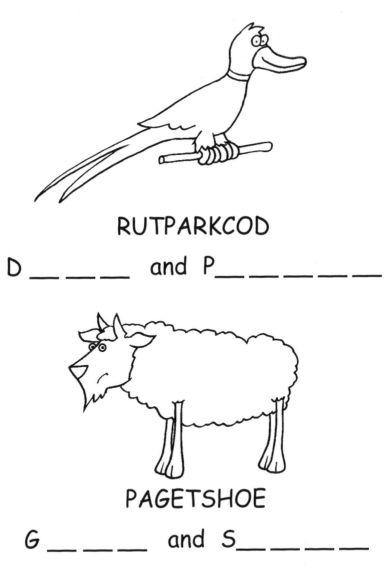

RUTPARKCOD

D __ __ __ and P__ __ __ __ __ __

PAGETSHOE

G __ __ __ and S__ __ __ __ __

Be a sport

Cross out all the pairs of letters that appear in the grid.
Use the remaining letters to spell a sport.

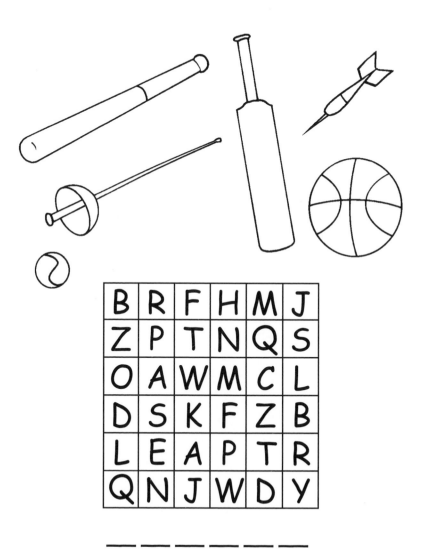

B	R	F	H	M	J
Z	P	T	N	Q	S
O	A	W	M	C	L
D	S	K	F	Z	B
L	E	A	P	T	R
Q	N	J	W	D	Y

_ _ _ _ _ _

On the beach

Finish the picture by adding some other creatures that have come to the beach today.

Home from home

Can you find five different types of dwelling using the letters in each word wheel? We've given you the first letter of each word to start you off.

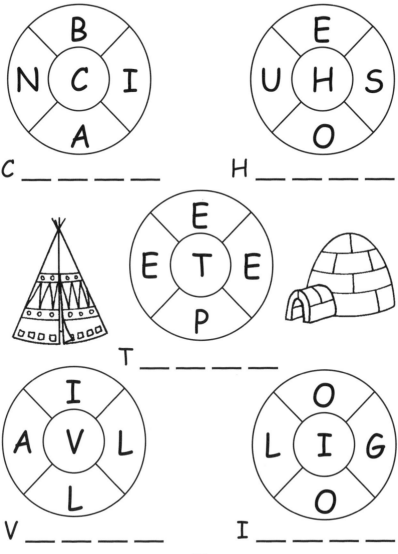

C _ _ _ _ _

H _ _ _ _ _

T _ _ _ _ _

V _ _ _ _ _

I _ _ _ _ _

Get away

Unscramble the letters to find four types of transport.

FATCHORVER

H _ _ _ _ _ _ _ _ _

OPENARALE

A _ _ _ _ _ _ _ _

CLICBYE

B _ _ _ _ _ _

ESCORTO

S _ _ _ _ _ _

Where's the hare?

Circle this bouncing hare's exact shadow.

World tour

Go globetrotting and find all these countries in the wordsearch grid.

CUBA
CHAD
ENGLAND
INDIA
CANADA
GREECE

SWEDEN
ITALY
JAPAN
SPAIN
FRANCE
NORWAY

```
E N G L A N D X E P
W G Y C A N A D A F
B C U B A E N G L I
S T M D J F O R A T
P A C H Q R R E B A
A I N D I A W E J L
I O Z C N N A C A Y
N H R H F C Y E P V
I U J A C E G S A K
S W E D E N M D N O
```

Fresh veg

All of these veggie words have been split into two syllables. Connect the two halves to complete each word.

car	snip
par	ish
lett	li
cabb	root
chil	uce
mush	rot
rad	age
beet	room

Do bears like honey?

Follow the trails to find out which bear gets the honey.

Fossil hunter

Start by crossing out the letter 'A' and then delete
alternate letters as you work your way through the list.
The remaining letters will reveal a dinosaur!

ASOTLE NGUOSS
DARUN RIURS

_ _ _ _ _ _ _ _ _ _ _ _ _

Face the music

Read the clues and complete the words using only vowels.

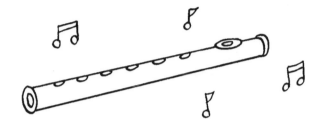

V __ __ L __ N   a stringed instrument

M __ S C __ __ N   a member of a group

C __ N D __ C T __ R   orchestra leader

S __ N G __ R   vocalist

T R __ M B __ N __   a brass instrument

P __ __ N __   a keyboard instrument

C __ N C __ R T   a musical performance

M __ S __ C __ L   a play with songs

In training

Can you spot the matching pair of trainers?

Dig this!

Count the number of letters in each word,
and then fit them into the crossword grid.

GARDEN   HEDGE   SPADE   FORK

FLOWER   SHED   LAWN   PATIO

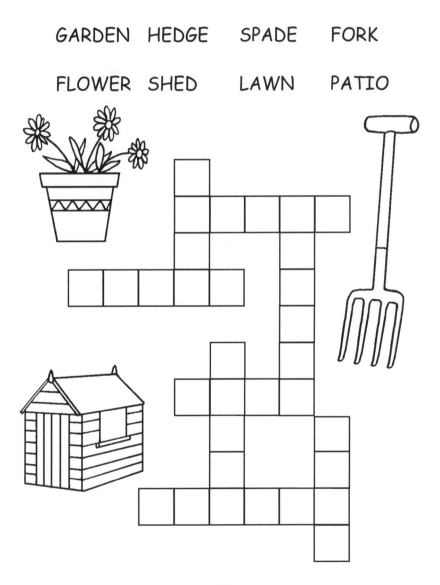

Link a word

Join the words with the pictures to create four new words.

book

leap

hand

light

Write the new words here.

_____   _____

_____   _____

Crowning glory!

This careless queen has gone and lost her crown!
Help her through the maze to find it.

Down under

Use the word square to crack the code and name a famous building in Sydney, Australia.

	a	b	c	d	e	f	g
1	L	O	Z	M	V	E	H
2	N	W	P	N	B	D	E
3	R	A	E	C	V	A	J
4	T	G	H	S	U	D	O
5	S	P	E	U	X	K	Q

Fill in the squares to name the building.

1b   2c   1f   3a   3f   4c   4g   5d   5a   2g

Slippery customers!

Unscramble the letters to find two types of snake in the first puzzle, and two amphibians in the second.

DRABARCODE

C _ _ _ _ _ _ and A_ _ _ _ _

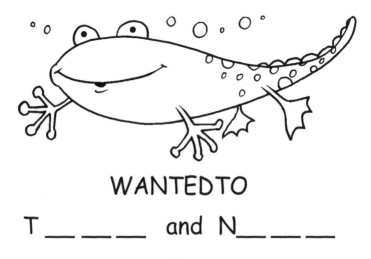

WANTEDTO

T _ _ _ and N_ _ _ _

Something fishy

Dive in and try to spot which goldfish bowl is different to the rest.

Frosty fun

Are you cool enough to find six differences between the pictures?

Where in the world?

Cross out all the pairs of letters that appear in the grid.
Use the remaining letters to spell a capital city.

R	H	X	A	C	P
E	D	K	F	O	S
U	A	J	T	H	B
T	Y	L	E	M	R
X	I	C	S	O	K
F	M	P	N	Y	J

— — — — — —

Fresh fruit

Can you find five different types of fruit using the letters in each word wheel? We've given you the first letter of each word to start you off.

A _ _ _ _ _

G _ _ _ _ _

P _ _ _ _ _

M _ _ _ _ _

M _ _ _ _ _

Fun farm

Finish the picture by drawing in the rest of Percy's farmyard friends.

A bug's life

Unscramble the letters to find four types of insect.

DRYBALDI

L _ _ _ _ _ _ _

CLEARILTRAP

C _ _ _ _ _ _ _ _ _ _

ETEBEL

B _ _ _ _ _

QUITSMOO

M _ _ _ _ _ _ _

Creepy crawlies!

All of these creepy crawlies are hiding in the wordsearch. Can you find them?

FLEA
SPIDER
WEEVIL
MIDGE
BEE
MITE

WASP
EARWIG
NIT
CRICKET
MOTH
HORNET

E	M	I	D	G	E	J	G	V	E
Q	F	B	H	O	R	N	E	T	A
W	Z	E	W	F	L	E	A	H	R
A	X	E	G	N	O	T	H	R	W
S	P	H	D	C	G	O	Y	K	I
P	D	A	S	P	I	D	E	R	G
U	I	T	J	B	K	N	M	M	S
C	R	I	C	K	E	T	N	I	T
E	I	C	E	L	D	F	L	T	A
W	E	E	V	I	L	M	B	E	F

Ship shape

One of these shadows exactly matches the ship.
But which one?

Party time!

All of these party words have been split into two syllables. Connect the two halves to complete each word.

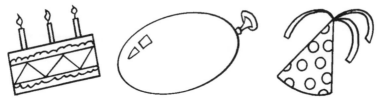

ball	rades
can	cing
pres	oon
birth	mer
dan	ic
mus	day
strea	ent
cha	dle

He's a hero

Start by crossing out the letter 'B' and then delete
alternate letters as you work your way through the list.
The remaining letters will reveal a legendary hero.

BRAOS BLIEN
THFO PONDE

___ ___ ___ ___ ___

___ ___ ___ ___

All downhill

Follow the trails to find out which skier wins the race.

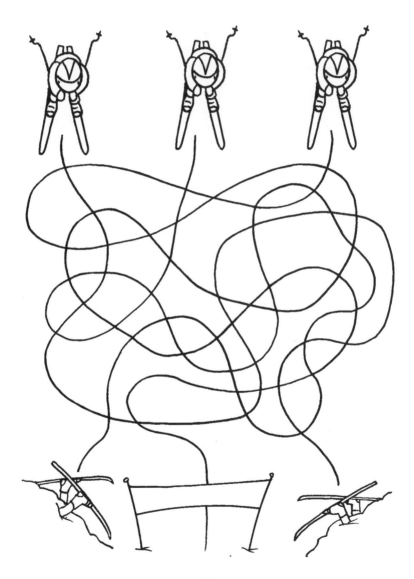

Happy holidays

Read the clues and complete the words using only vowels.

__ __ R P __ R T   a place to fly from

S __ __ T C __ S __   baggage

T __ C K __ T   travel voucher

S __ N D __ L S   beach shoes

B __ __ C H   seashore

V __ Y __ G __   sea journey

S K __ __ N G   winter sport

C __ R R __ N C Y   foreign money

On safari

Count the number of letters in each word,
and then fit them into the crossword grid.

GIRAFFE LION RHINO ELEPHANT

LEOPARD HIPPO ZEBRA HYENA

Scarecrow search

Only two of these scarecrows are identical.
Can you spot them?

Two make one

Join the pictures with the words to create four new words.

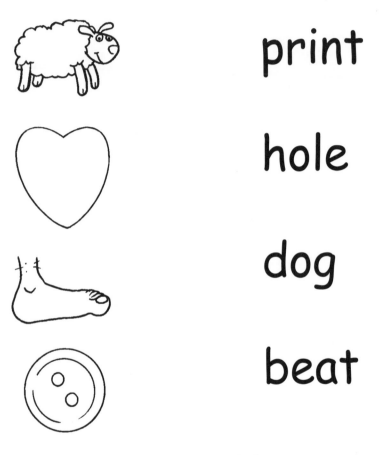

print

hole

dog

beat

Write the new words here.

_____   _____

_____   _____

Rule the waves

Use the word square to crack the code and name the Roman god of the sea.

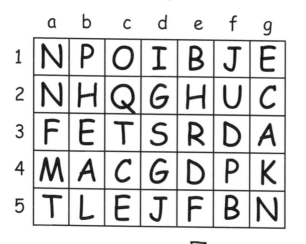

	a	b	c	d	e	f	g
1	N	P	O	I	B	J	E
2	N	H	Q	G	H	U	C
3	F	E	T	S	R	D	A
4	M	A	C	G	D	P	K
5	T	L	E	J	F	B	N

Fill in the squares to name the god.

1a 3b 4f 5a 2f 5g 1g

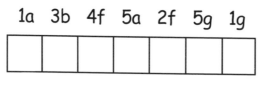

Slowcoach

Lead this slowcoach tortoise through the maze to reach his favourite lettuce leaf before it turns bad!

Head to toe

Unscramble the letters to find two hats in the first puzzle, and two types of footwear in the second.

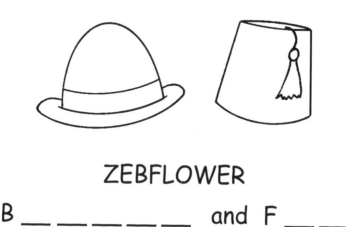

ZEBFLOWER

B _ _ _ _ _ _ and F _ _

BOPLIERPOST

S _ _ _ _ _ _ _ and B _ _ _ _

Reach the heights!

Help the mountaineers reach the summit by spotting six differences between the pictures.

Munch-munch

Which one of these hungry caterpillars is
not quite the same as the others?

So sweet!

Cross out all the pairs of letters that appear in the grid.
Use the remaining letters to spell a cake.

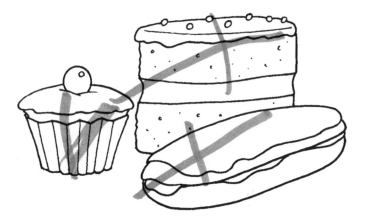

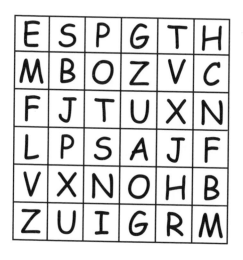

E	S	P	G	T	H
M	B	O	Z	V	C
F	J	T	U	X	N
L	P	S	A	J	F
V	X	N	O	H	B
Z	U	I	G	R	M

_ _ _ _ _ _ _

Find a fish

Can you find five different types of fish using the letters in each word wheel? We've given you the first letter of each word to start you off.

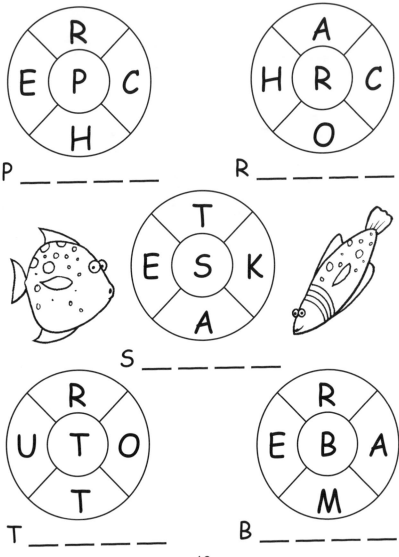

P _ _ _ _ _

R _ _ _ _ _

S _ _ _ _ _

T _ _ _ _ _

B _ _ _ _ _

High in the sky

Draw in the crazy-looking kites being flown by this couple.

In colour

Unscramble the letters to reveal four cool colours.

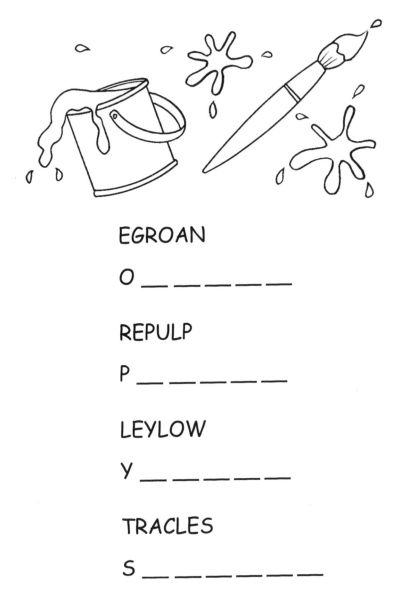

EGROAN

O __ __ __ __ __

REPULP

P __ __ __ __ __

LEYLOW

Y __ __ __ __ __

TRACLES

S __ __ __ __ __ __

Out of this world

Find the exact shadow of this visiting alien.

Making music

Drum roll please! Can you find all the musical instruments in the wordsearch?

DRUM
OBOE
PIANO
FLUTE
CYMBAL
BASSOON

CELLO
GUITAR
VIOLIN
HARP
HORN
TUBA

V G T U B A G Q B E
I D R U M H U S A P
O R F A O D I B S C
L Z N F L U T E S E
I M Y C H D A C O L
N E H L H A R P O L
O B O E F O V I N O
A T R N L G K B W I
U M N J P P I A N O
C Y M B A L Q K X J

Yo-ho-ho!

All of these pirate-themed words have been split into two syllables. Connect the two halves to complete each word.

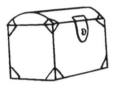  

par	land
cut	boat
eye	ver
can	rot
long	patch
sil	chor
is	lass
an	non

Into the frying pan

Follow the trails to find out which pancake lands back in the frying pan.

What's in the box?

Start by crossing out the letter 'S' and then delete alternate letters as you work your way through the list. The remaining letters will reveal a large insect.

STWAL REABNO

TFUP LUAN

_ _ _ _ _ _ _ _ _ _

Feathered friends

Read the clues and complete the words using only vowels.

__ S T R __ C H   a large, flightless bird

R __ B __ N   redbreast

__ L B __ T R __ S S   a sea bird

P __ R R __ T   an exotic bird

__ __ G L __   a bird of prey

C __ N __ R Y   a yellow bird

V __ L T __ R __   a large, carrion bird

F L __ M __ N G __   a pink bird

Spaced out

Search through space to find the two astronauts that are exactly the same.

Bird watch

Count the number of letters in each word,
and then fit them into the crossword grid.

FALCON   PEACOCK   FINCH   GULL

ROBIN   SPARROW   CURLEW   TERN

Join them together

Join the pictures with the words to create four new words.

glasses

shell

fare

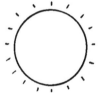

girl

Write the new words here.

_____   _____

_____   _____

Going gnome

The nutty gnome needs to sit down but he has
forgotten where his favourite toadstool is.
Can you lead him through the maze to find it?

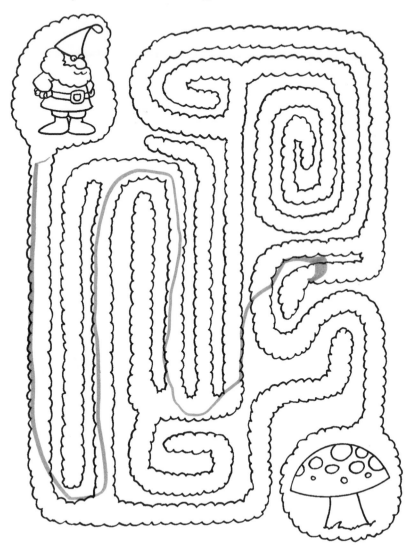

Where am I?

Use the word square to crack the code and name a mountainous country in Europe.

	a	b	c	d	e	f	g
1	L	K	W	X	H	L	J
2	S	Y	M	B	W	Q	R
3	C	D	A	G	I	M	N
4	Z	N	T	A	C	O	U
5	Z	K	V	P	X	E	F

Fill in the squares to name the country.

2a 1c 3e 4c 5a 5f 2g 1f 4d 3g 3b

In the woods

Unscramble the letters to find two types of tree in the first puzzle, and two woodland creatures in the second.

CHUNKETOAST

C _ _ _ _ _ _ _ _ _ and O_ _

QUILWORSLER

S_ _ _ _ _ _ _ _ and O_ _

Mission control

Take a space walk to find which one of these
rockets is the odd one out?

And the winner is...

It's a race to find six differences between this picture and the one on the facing page?

Up in the air

Cross out all the pairs of letters that appear in the grid.
Use the remaining letters to spell an aircraft.

C	P	J	K	U	G
A	Y	F	W	T	N
O	L	S	I	M	B
P	N	D	T	C	Y
J	B	U	F	O	S
E	A	K	W	M	R

__ __ __ __ __ __

Let's dance

Can you find five different types of dance using the letters in each word wheel? We've given you the first letter of each word to start you off.

D _ _ _ _ _

R _ _ _ _ _

S _ _ _ _ _

W _ _ _ _ _

P _ _ _ _

Beep-beep!

Who has taken the car for a spin in the countryside?
Do a doodle and decide!

In translation

Unscramble the letters to reveal four languages.

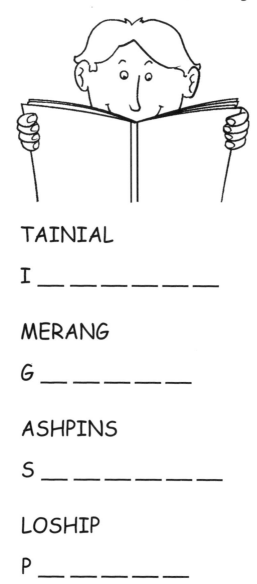

TAINIAL

I _ _ _ _ _ _

MERANG

G _ _ _ _ _

ASHPINS

S _ _ _ _ _ _

LOSHIP

P _ _ _ _ _

Body bits

You can find all these bits on your body... but can you find them in the wordsearch?

ARM   LEG
HAND   KNEE
FOOT   TOE
SKULL   FINGER
NAILS   ELBOW
HAIR   EYES

```
G E L B O W H M F L
U K H O F O O T I E
H T N I L E G V C G
A R M E N A I L S L
N S E Y E S J K B M
D S F J W K N E E D
B Q X A Y P N C V R
Y S K U L L Z U D T
O T P R H A I R Q O
F I N G E R X W A E
```

Which witch?

Circle the shadow that exactly matches this wacky witch.

By the sea

All of these seaside words have been split into two syllables. Connect the two halves to complete each word.

rock	cream
star	ball
light	board
beach	house
ice	dals
san	weed
surf	pool
sea	fish

That's a pasta

Start by crossing out the letter 'O' and then delete alternate letters as you work your way through the list. The remaining letters will reveal a type of pasta.

OTLAN GULSIN

AFTREX LULGE

_ _ _ _ _ _ _ _ _ _ _ _

It's a goal!

Follow the trails to find out which player scores the goal.

Food for thought

Read the clues and complete the words using only vowels.

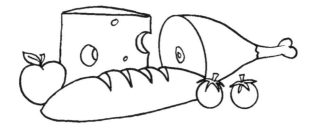

P __ T __ T __   a vegetable

R __ V __ __ L __   a type of pasta

C H __ W D __ R   fish soup

B R __ W N __ __   chocolate cake

S T __ __ K   a type of beef

Y __ G H __ R T   curdled milk

C __ F __   a place to eat

C __ __ B __ T T __   an Italian bread

Thirsty work

Count the number of letters in each word,
and then fit them into the crossword grid.

TEA   COFFEE   MILK   WATER

COLA   JUICE   COCOA   LEMONADE

Knight time

Two knights are exactly the same – but which ones?

Make four words

Join the words with the pictures to create four new words.

space

jig

toad

sauce

Write the new words here.

_____   _____

_____   _____

Big cheese

Use the word square to crack the code and name the heaviest land animal.

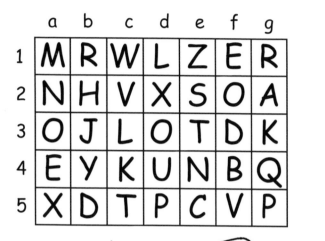

	a	b	c	d	e	f	g
1	M	R	W	L	Z	E	R
2	N	H	V	X	S	O	A
3	O	J	L	O	T	D	K
4	E	Y	K	U	N	B	Q
5	X	D	T	P	C	V	P

Fill in the squares to name the animal.

1f   3c   4a   5g   2b   2g   4e   5c

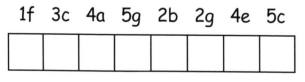

Feather your nest

Our little feathered friend needs to get back to her nest. Work out the quickest route to the eggs before they hatch!

Sporting chance

Unscramble the letters to find two types of sport in the first puzzle, and two board games in the second.

FLINTSGONE

T _ _ _ _ _ _ _   and G _ _ _ _

SHECLOUDS

C _ _ _ _ _   and L _ _ _

A dog's life

This muddy mutt is having a bath! Can you spot six differences between the two pictures?

Come out of your shell

Cross out all the pairs of letters that appear in the grid.
Use the remaining letters to spell a shellfish.

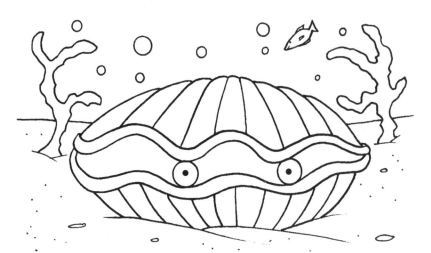

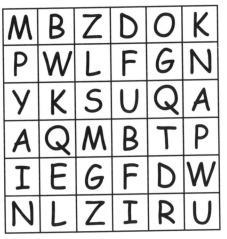

M	B	Z	D	O	K
P	W	L	F	G	N
Y	K	S	U	Q	A
A	Q	M	B	T	P
I	E	G	F	D	W
N	L	Z	I	R	U

— — — — — —

Hop to it

Which of these croakers is slightly different
to the others?

Beautiful blooms

Can you find five different types of flower using the letters in each word wheel? We've given you the first letter of each word to start you off.

D _ _ _ _ _

P _ _ _ _ _

T _ _ _ _

L _ _ _ _ _

P _ _ _ _ _

What a gem!

Unscramble the letters to reveal four gemstones.

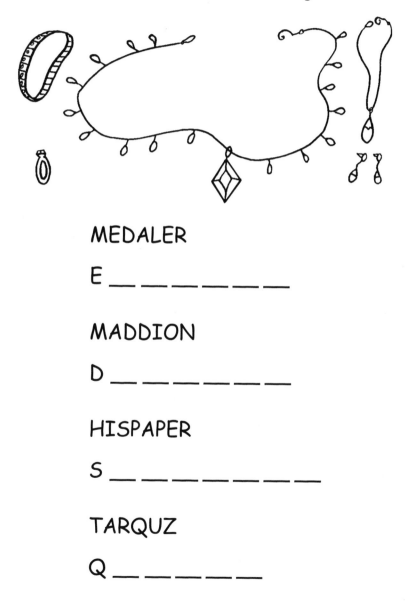

MEDALER

E _ _ _ _ _ _

MADDION

D _ _ _ _ _ _

HISPAPER

S _ _ _ _ _ _ _

TARQUZ

Q _ _ _ _ _

Fishy fun

Finish the picture by drawing in the rest of sharky's pals in this underwater scene.

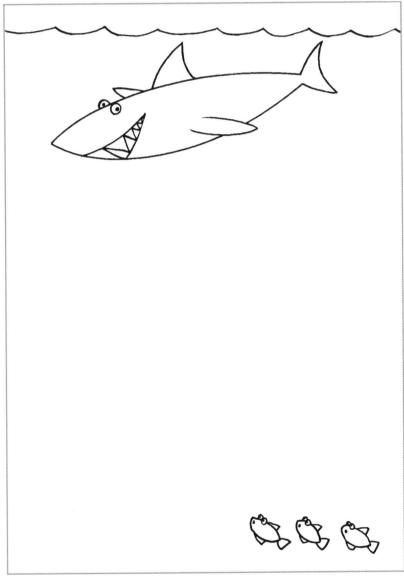

On the move

Get your skates on and find twelve vehicles
hidden in the wordsearch.

BOAT   KART

SHIP   TRUCK

BICYCLE   TRAIN

AIRCRAFT   SLEDGE

SLEIGH   BUS

TRAM   CAR

```
B  P  E  K  X  O  S  H  I  P
I  B  O  A  T  Y  G  S  C  Z
C  N  W  R  T  U  B  L  F  S
Y  G  A  T  R  U  C  K  M  L
C  Q  D  F  I  C  H  K  C  E
L  B  T  R  A  I  N  V  B  D
E  N  H  O  J  P  A  K  U  G
R  S  L  E  I  G  H  L  S  E
E  I  T  R  A  M  Q  A  B  D
A  I  R  C  R  A  F  T  J  M
```

In the woods

All of these words have been split into two syllables.
Connect the two halves to complete each word.

  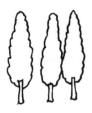

pop	ow
haw	berry
chest	thorn
will	wood
cher	lar
ma	nut
red	ry

Must fly

Catch the fly by circling his exact shadow.

Building work

Start by crossing out the letter 'P' and then delete alternate letters as you work your way through the list. The remaining letters will reveal an occupation.

PANRUC THFIL
TSEK CATO

_ _ _ _ _ _ _ _ _ _

Space race

Read the clues and complete the words using only vowels.

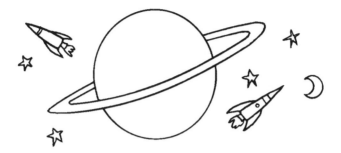

M __ __ N   the earth's satellite

R __ C K __ T   space transport

__ L __ __ N   a being from outer space

M __ R S   the red planet

S __ T __ R N   a planet with rings

__ __ R T H   our planet

__ C L __ P S __   the moon hiding the sun

G __ L __ X Y   a large group of stars

Bullseye!

Follow the trails to find out which arrow hits the target.

Nice and spicy

Count the number of letters in each word,
and then fit them into the crossword grid.

PARSLEY   BASIL   PAPRIKA DILL

CINNAMON THYME   CHILLI   MINT

Split words

Join the words with the pictures to create four new words.

rattle

arm

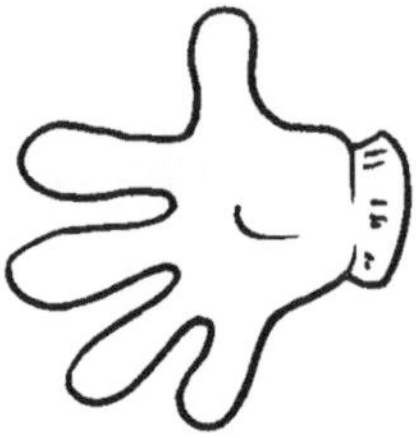

rain

fox

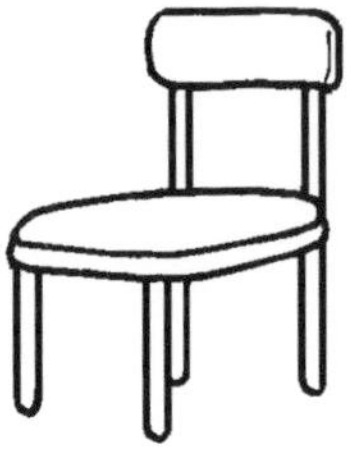

Write the new words here.

_____   _____

_____   _____

Twin terriers

Spot the two scottie dogs that are identical.

My hero!

Use the word square to crack the code and name a comic book superhero.

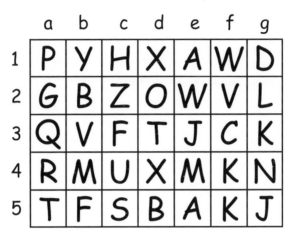

Fill in the squares to name the superhero.

2b   1e   3d   4b   5e   4g

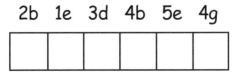

Who are you?

Unscramble the letters to find two occupations in the first puzzle, and two girl's names in the second.

DOPORTCRUMBLE

D__ __ __ __ __ and P__ __ __ __ __ __ __ __

AHASTYKAR

K __ __ __ and S__ __ __ __

Happy birthday!

Alice needs help through the maze to get to her birthday present. Lead the way and make it a really happy day.

First prize

Cross out all the pairs of letters that appear in the grid.
Use the remaining letters to spell a prize.

A	X	K	T	E	S
I	F	C	J	A	L
R	N	Q	O	V	D
L	P	E	H	M	K
V	S	D	X	N	F
C	J	M	I	Y	Q

— — — — — —

Very bunny!

The bunnies are bouncing this morning but can you spot six differences between the pictures?

Answers

Page 4

Page 5
CANOE   DINGY
SCULL   YACHT
BARGE

Page 6
BLOODHOUND   LABRADOR
DALMATION   SPANIEL

Page 8
```
  V   J      S  M
NEPTUNE   I  E
  N   P      R  R
  U   I      I  C
   SSATURNU  U
P     E    S    R
L   URANUS Y
UPOLE
T  EARTH
OMIRA  MARS
```

Page 9
PENCIL   HOMEWORK
WHITEBOARD   CLASSROOM
TEACHER   PLAYGROUND
BACKPACK   LESSONS

Page 10

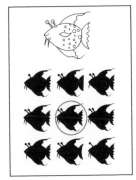

Page 11
BLACK BEAUTY

Page 12

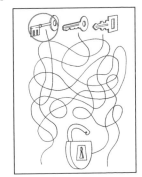

Page 13
GIRAFFE
CAMEL
CHEETAH
AARDVARK
KANGAROO
BABOON
PANDA
MOOSE

Answers

Page 14

```
        H
      A   J
    T I E
          A
          N
  P Y J A M A S
      A
        C O A T
  S     K
G L O V E S
      C   T
      K
```

Page 18

Page 15

Page 19

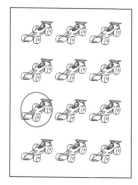

Page 16
HORSESHOE
HONEYBEE
FLOWERBED
PAINTBRUSH

Page 17
LANCELOT

Page 20–21

Answers

Page 22

DUCK   PARROT

GOAT   SHEEP

Page 23

HOCKEY

Page 25

CABIN   HOUSE

TEPEE   VILLA

IGLOO

Page 26

HOVERCRAFT   AEROPLANE

BICYCLE   SCOOTER

Page 27

Page 28

```
EN GLA ND
       CANADA
   CUBA  NG    I
 S        FOR   T
 P        R RE  A
 A INDIAWEJ L
 I    C NAC A Y
 N    H CYE P
       A E    A
 SWEDEN    N
```

Page 29

CARROT   PARSNIP

LETTUCE   CABBAGE

CHILLI   MUSHROOM

RADISH   BEETROOT

Page 30

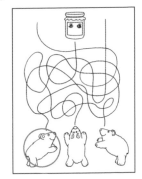

Page 31

STEGOSAURUS

Page 32

VIOLIN   MUSCIAN

CONDUCTOR   SINGER

TROMBONE   PIANO

CONCERT   MUSICAL

Page 33

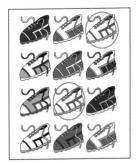

120

Answers

Page 34

```
    S
    H E D G E
    E       A
S P A D E   R
        P   D
        P   E
    L A W N
        T       F
        I       O
    F L O W E R
                K
```

Page 35

BOOKWORM   LEAPFROG
HANDBAG   LIGHTHOUSE

Page 36

Page 37

OPERA HOUSE

Page 38

COBRA
ADDER
TOAD
NEWT

Page 39

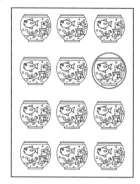

Page 40–41

Page 42

DUBLIN

Page 43

APPLE   GRAPE
PEACH   MELON
MANGO

Page 45

LADYBIRD   CATERPILLAR
BEETLE   MOSQUITO

Answers

Page 46

```
  M I D G E      E
      B H O R N E T A
W   E   F L E A    R
A   E              W
S                  I
P     S P I D E R  G
          M
C R I C K E T N I T
            T
W E E V I L   E
```

Page 47

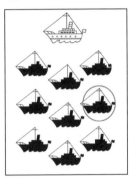

Page 48

BALLOON
CANDLES
PRESENTS
BIRTHDAY
DANCING
MUSIC
STREAMER
CHARADES

Page 49

ROBIN HOOD

Page 50

Page 51

AIRPORT
SUITCASE
TICKET
SANDALS
BEACH
VOYAGE
SKIING
CURRENCY

Page 52

```
      E L E P H A N T
              I
        L E O P A R D
              P
      R H I N O
      Y
      Z E B R A
    L   N
  G I R A F F E
  O
  N
```

Answers

Page 53

Page 54

SHEEPDOG   HEARTBEAT
FOOTPRINT   BUTTONHOLE

Page 55
NEPTUNE

Page 56

Page 57

BOWLER   FEZ
SLIPPER   BOOT

Page 58–59

Page 60

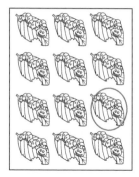

Page 61
ÉCLAIR

Page 62

PERCH   ROACH
SKATE   TROUT
BREAM

Page 64

ORANGE   PURPLE
YELLOW   SCARLET

Answers

```
V   T U B A G   B
I D R U M   U A
O           I SC
L       F L U T E S E
I           A  O L
N  H     H A R P O L
O B O E         N O
   R
   N     P I A N O
C Y  M B A L
```

PARROT
CUTLASS
EYEPATCH
CANNON
LONGBOAT
SILVER
ISLAND
ANCHOR

TARANTULA

OSTRICH
ROBIN
ALBATROSS
PARROT
EAGLE
CANARY
VULTURE
FLAMINGO

Answers

Page 72

```
        P
        E     R
    S P A R R O W
        C     B
        O     I
    F I N C H  N
    A     K
G U L L
    C U R L E W
    O
T E R N
```

Page 73

COWGIRL   FANFARE
SUNGLASSES EGGSHELL

Page 74

Page 75

SWITZERLAND

Page 76

CHESTNUT   OAK
SQUIRREL   OWL

Page 77

Page 78-79

Page 80

GLIDER

Page 81

DISCO   RUMBA
SAMBA   WALTZ
POLKA

Page 83

ITALIAN   GERMAN
SPANISH   POLISH

Answers

Page 84

```
  E L B O W      L
        F O O T E
H               G
A R M   N A I L S
N   E Y E S
D         K N E E

  S K U L L      T
      H A I R    O
F I N G E R      E
```

Page 85

Page 86

ROCKPOOL   STARFISH
LIGHTHOUSE   BEACHBALL
ICECREAM   SANDALS
SURFBOARD   SEAWEED

Page 87

TAGLIATELLE

Page 88

Page 89

PATATO   RAVIOLI
CHOWDER   BROWNIE
STEAK   YOGHURT
CAFÉ   CIABATTA

Page 90

```
C O C O A
O   O       J
  F   L     U
  F   A   M I L K
  E     W   C
L E M O N A D E
          T
        T E A
        R
```

Page 91

Page 92

SPACESHIP   JIGSAW
TOADSTOOL   SAUCEPAN

Page 93

ELEPHANT

Answers

Page 94

Page 95

TENNIS   GOLF
CHESS   LUDO

Page 96-97

Page 98
OYSTER

Page 99

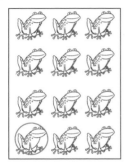

Page 100
DAISY   PANSY
TULIP   LUPIN
POPPY

Page 101
EMERALD   DIAMOND
SAPPHIRE   QUARTZ

Page 103
```
B    K     SHIP
IBOAT        C
C    R      A S
Y     TRUCK R L
C           E
L TRAIN   B D
E         U G
  SLEIGH  S E
   TRAM
AIRCRAFT
```

Page 104
POPLAR   HAWTHORN
CHESTNUT   WILLOW
CHERRY   MAPLE
REDWOOD   MULBERRY

Page 105

Page 106
ARCHITECT

127

Answers

Page 107

MOON   ROCKET
ALIEN   MARS
SATURN EARTH
ECLIPSE GALAXY

Page 108

Page 109

```
            T
            H   C
  P A R S L E Y   I
  A           M I N T
  P     C     E     N
  R     H           A
  I  D I L L        M
  K     L           O
B A S I L            N
        I
```

Page 110

RATTLESNAKE ARMCHAIR
RAINBOW   FOXGLOVE

Page 111

Page 112
BATMAN

Page 113
DOCTOR PLUMBER
KATY   SARAH

Page 114

Page 115
TROPHY

Page 116–117